I0145715

The Enlightened Teacher
Vignettes to Guide Your Practice

Patty Lee, Ed. D.

Copyright © 2013, Patty Lee, Ed. D.

All rights reserved.
No part of this document may be reproduced, stored in
a retrieval system, or transmitted by any means,
electronic, mechanical, photocopying, recording, or
otherwise, without written permission
from the author.

First Printing May 2014
By
Sojourn Publishing, LLC.

ISBN 978-1-62747-026-1
e-ISBN 978-1-62747-027-8

Contents

Forward

I have been in the field of education for almost twenty years, and while I have never believed the vocation of education is for the faint of heart, it is with increasing concern that I wonder at any teacher's ability to sustain their commitment, passion, and joy for this profession. But it is educators like Dr. Patty Lee, who has not only sustained these but has also dedicated her career to helping educators connect and reconnect to the purpose of our pathways, that nurtures my hopes for the future of teachers and all of the students whose lives they touch.

I have had the privilege of being witness and learner to Patty's role as a teacher and mentor of teachers. Central to her own way of being, and that which she fosters among others, is reflection as a teaching practice. Patty has also taught me the importance of trusting the truths of our own inner voices, and of creating spaces in which the wisdom of all voices is given an opportunity to be heard. As Patty's colleague, I came to recognize how critical it is that we not surrender to the sense of loneliness and isolation, but rather we must find ways to share our feelings, experiences, and our stories as a means to learn, to heal, to celebrate, and to sustain our passion for teaching.

If you choose to embark on a journey of reflecting upon the why and the how of your teaching practice with this book, you will surely gain what I have in my relationship with Patty: a mentor who asks questions to support learning and growth, a coach cheering you on from the sidelines, a caring colleague who holds up a mirror, a wise guide without judgment or blame, and a friend, who at the end of a long and frustrating week listens with empathy as you rail against the injustices of the system and patiently waits for just the right moment to ask, "So what can you do now to create your path within this?"

"It's time," as Patty shares, "to step back and look at your teaching path and ask yourself if you're heading down the road that will take you to the teacher you long to become." It is a journey you will find well worth the time, as one that will reconnect you to why it is you have chosen this profession and the ways in which you can make the difference you want to make.

Dr. Erica Volkers, Dean
Central New Mexico Community College

In Gratitude

Thanks to

- All the teachers I have known over the years who have been courageous enough to share their stories
- Miss Loudermilk, my 5th grade teacher who probably knew I was "over the moon" for her
- Dr. Gordon Alley, for seeing, hearing and challenging the real me
- Denzel, for being my true friend and confidant
- Aaron Stern, for trusting me
- Tom Bird, for waking up the sleeping author within
- Rama, for his unflagging kindness and support
- Mom, Dad and Billy Jay,
  and
- Judy, the spice of my life!

Introduction

So this is for you, dear teachers—teachers who take the weight of the world through the children you meet every day—for the life you have chosen, for the profession that has chosen you. This book is a companion you can turn to anytime; first thing in the morning, maybe even in the middle of your day, or just before you say good night. Something to remind you of why you came into this teaching world in the first place, why you chose to spend your days in a place called school.

This guided journal is meant to get you out of the *form* and into the *function* of learning. That's what you came here for—to be in the center of learning. Maybe you loved being in school yourself and wanted to bring that love to others; or maybe you had lousy teachers, and you wanted to be sure you never treated your students the way you had been treated. In some sense, you wanted to make a difference, and you chose school as your place to do that.

And what have you found? Perhaps you've found that the school climate is radically different than you expected.

You may find yourself among colleagues who seem as if they do not like what they are doing, and may even have a distaste for students. Odd but true. Or you experience administrators who are far more interested in how quiet your students are than what and how they are learning.

No matter the climate in which you find yourself, it's time to get back to YOUR reason for becoming a teacher. It's time to step back and look at your teaching path and ask yourself if you're heading down the road that will take you to the teacher you long to become. Are you living full out in this profession or holding back? What do you think might fill the void? Most importantly, what will serve the larger purpose of your teaching life?

It has been nearly fifty years that I have been in one school or another. Throughout most of this time, I have served as teacher and as witness. I've been fascinated by what it is that causes some teachers to stay and thrive, some to leave and others to remain on the job as cynics and victims. The vignettes in this book are the result of what I have seen, what I have wondered, and what I hold as my deepest desire for teachers.

Each vignette is meant to be savored for a day, a week, or whatever your schedule allows. Open to any page or take it in the order it is written. Use the open space on each page for your thoughts, intentions, and dreams. May these lessons connect you with your true teacher self and give you pause to understand the story you are living as a teacher.

In the spirit of learning,
Patty Lee, Ed. D.

The system is not there to nurture you...

You cannot count on the system to support your dream as a teacher; you may have to find nurturance elsewhere. It will come in those moments of "aha" when students' eyes light up with understanding. It will come in those times of collaboration with a colleague where you know you are not alone. And it can come in unexpected glimpses of the truth we are.

The system is meant to run on forms, meant to be a well-honed machine; YOU ARE NOT THAT. The system can be full of doublespeak that espouses one thing and behaves another. Saying, "We want all students to reach their full potential," and then implementing practices that prohibit that possibility is for crazy making. You must trust yourself and what you know and not lose that compass.

You know about how children learn. You know about meaningful moments in the classroom. You know what the system does not know, so why would you give in to an authority that is not meant to sustain wisdom, that is there to simply keep the machine going? You can break the cycle and build for yourself an unending reservoir of sustainability. Take a look in the mirror and remember with all your heart the passion you have for this profession. Carry that with you today. Tuck it into your heart and trust its ancient wisdom.

Use the space below to identify the dysfunction in your particular system, and do what you can to let it be, realizing it has always been.

....
....
....
....
....
....
....
....
....
....
....

The job is infinite...

You are not. Your energy can be renewed, but it is finite and it behooves all of us to know what feeds us and what depletes us. The enormity of teaching is stunning. We will never have the flawless lesson plan; we will never be able to meet all of their individual needs; and we will come up forever short of total satisfaction with our craft. So what is it we *can* do? What will serve our path of learning as we teach?

Do you remember the movie, *What About Bob?* with Richard Dreyfuss and Bill Murray? The moral of Bob's story is that difficult change often comes about by taking baby steps. You don't expect your friend to have it all together all the time nor get it totally right. Perhaps you can befriend yourself and give yourself a needed break.

Use the space below to remind yourself, as you would a friend, that small steps make the journey. As John Denver sang, *"Some days are diamonds, some days are dust."* Find ways to savor the diamonds more and brush off the dust. Name the classroom moments that bring you absolute delight. This practice will help you find a bit of renewal and respite along the way.

Patty Lee, Ed. D.

....
....
....
....
....
....
....
....
....
....
....
....
....
....
....
....
....
....
....

Remembering your mentors

When I heard Maya Angelou read her poem "And Still I Rise," I knew that I had found a lifelong mentor. Somehow, I heard my story in hers and knew I was up to the task. If she could rise again after extreme abuse and discrimination, certainly I could get up again after being chastised by my principal. Recently I watched Dr. Angelou with Oprah, and I still find that her voice, her deep conviction, and her devotion stir me to tears. We all need these mentors in our lives—guides who point us toward our higher selves, who will not "settle," inspiring us to do the same.

Who are your mentors? Whose writing, art, dancing, or speaking brings you back into deep connection with your soulful self? Maybe a teacher you had in school who encouraged you beyond your own expectations, or an artist whose work continually inspires you to a peaceful and hopeful place. Find them once again and let their teaching get inside you. Let them provide soul food that will sustain you, for their lives are our lives. Call to mind your mentors and write their names in the space below. What characteristics or

values do they embody that inspires you toward the person
you are becoming?

....

....

....

....

....

....

....

....

....

....

....

....

....

....

....

....

Just try to fit in...

It is an interesting beginning that many teachers experience as they enter the profession. We finally get the job, go to the school with barely containable excitement, get our room and class assignment, and then are pretty much left alone to figure it out. It is this lack of orientation that may begin a lonely and isolated path for some teachers. An underlying and unspoken message seems to be, *"We're all pretty busy here. It would be great if you look around, see what others are doing, and just fit in."*

Teachers reaching out to teachers may not be the norm in your school. Everyone seems to be in their own classrooms with their own students and their own lessons to deliver. Schools are focused on creating communities of students and are often overlooking the community of teachers that is possible. When teachers *are* together in a large group, it is usually a staff meeting where the agenda is created by someone else or a professional development workshop where everyone is learning some new content (or one more thing that they *must* do). With this separated environment, it may be easy to just keep to yourself and do the best you can. I visited a private girls' school in Santa Fe recently, and a new teacher was feeling somewhat inadequate about her teaching methods. She commented she hoped she could just "fake it until she makes it."

If any of this rings true, and you find your path is somewhat lonely, wondering if others are experiencing some of the same ups and downs that you are, take heart and know that they probably are. In the teacher support groups that I lead, this is a common comment: *"I thought I was the only one."*

When teachers find that others are having similar experiences and feelings, camaraderie develops, stories are shared, and healing begins. Maybe you can break the ice by reaching out to another colleague and begin a conversation about a lesson you are planning, an incident in your classroom, or a project you want to brainstorm about. You can take a first step to interrupt the isolation cycle among teachers by this simple gesture, and I think you will be surprised at the gratification it provides.

As an old Chinese proverb counsels:

"A single conversation with a wise man is better than ten years of study."

So while you may have paid a lot to learn a lot in school, what you can glean from your colleagues in a few minutes is priceless.

Consider something you'd like to talk about with a colleague and jot your ideas here.

....

....

....

....

....

....

....

....

....

What we CAN do is what matters...

The research (and common sense) is clear: we all do better when we are in touch with our strengths, our power, and our talents. In fact, we're taught in our Teacher Preparation programs to help students find their strengths and build on them. Then there's the reality of what goes on in schools. The attention is often focused on what is wrong, what is abnormal, and what is not compliant. Who is out of line, talking too loudly, NOT turning in their assignments, and going against the grain? When we educate students in such large groups, the emphasis becomes management rather than learning.

Maybe your classroom can be different. Think about what it is that YOU do really well and pay attention to that today. Maybe you're a good listener. Perhaps you are skilled at asking good questions. See if you can do that even better today. Practicing what comes naturally to you and making it even better can be so rewarding. And so it is for your students. When you identify a gift or talent they seem to exhibit, see if you can follow up by asking them to demonstrate that talent again and in different ways, always striving for the best they can do.

Martha Graham expressed it beautifully when she reminded us that there is only one of each of us, and if we do not develop that unique gift, it will be lost to the world. Imagine what classrooms would look and feel like if, once a day, a student was trying to improve upon something they were already good at and doing something they loved to do.

When my colleague at the University of Northern Colorado came to me and said, "These students can't write," complaining she was not seeing the skills she expected them to have and coming from a point of blame, I took a deep breath and responded, "Then help them." I believe that's what teachers are meant to do.

In the space below, write the gifts and talents your students have, and then pay attention to how they can develop them further. If you are unsure, perhaps you can devise ways of finding out. Have fun becoming acquainted with your students through their natural abilities. Invite them to show what they know.

....

....

....

....

....

....

....

....

....

....

....

....

....

....

....

....

....

....

....

In what do we trust?

As teachers, we certainly want our classrooms to be communities of trust. The question is: how is trust developed, manifested, and sustained? Deborah Meier, in her book *In Schools We Trust* (2002), posits that when teachers show themselves as willing to be learners alongside their students, a climate of trust is possible. On the other hand, when teachers feel they must always have the answer, always be a model of doing things "right," the children in their presence come to feel unsure about themselves and less willing to take a risk.

So how do you demonstrate you are a learner alongside your students? If they know *you* are still figuring some things out and still having doubts about an answer, the safety net expands. You want them safe enough to take risks, okay with not knowing, and sure they will not be put on the spot at these vulnerable times.

You can begin by watching yourself, becoming aware of what you do in the presence of your students when *you* do not know something. Let them know what you are learning, where you just made a mistake, and how that made you feel. Take note of how often you feel *with* your students rather than *at* or *over* them. Meier counsels that when you convey that the classroom is a community of presumed equals learning together, you will be planting seeds of trust.

Think of the teachers you have had and the various levels of trust you experienced in school. How did you feel in their different classrooms? In whose presence did you trust yourself as a learner?

....

....

....

....

....

....

....

....

....

....

How'd I do?

Remember when you were in school and your teacher was getting ready to hand the papers back. Do you remember the feeling you had? Did you anticipate the marks and comments added to your paper? Did you feel the humility and shame I did when I was in the fifth grade? Having been one of the best spellers in class, I was absolutely humiliated when my teacher called me up to the front of the class to get my spelling test on that slim piece of lined paper. She simply said to me, "*Here you are, buzy*"...as I had misspelled the word "busy" using a "z" instead of "s." I know I must have turned beet red as I walked to the front of the class to get the paper. All the times I had gotten a 100% had no power now. I was simply a bad speller, missing one word out of the royal 20.

What do I wish had happened? Well, I think feedback should be pretty personal and pretty private between teacher and student. I think I should have known what I did correctly and the mistake I made in writing "buzy." That's all. I don't think she should have called everyone's attention to me.

Let's think about how feedback informs, how it might hurt, and how it might help. When you as teacher can make a comment on my paper about what I wrote and what the effect was, then I learn. This tells me so much more than "good job!" For example, meaningful feedback might go something like:

"When you started the paragraph with the words 'All is well,' it made me curious about what was to come. It caught my attention. On the other hand, when you began your paragraph with, 'The time didn't make it right,' I was confused and didn't know what you meant."

When students receive feedback in this form, describing what the student did and the effect it had on the reader or listener, it is instructional and respectful.

Use the space below to practice feedback statements you can give, so that students will know what they did and the impact it had.

....
....
....
....
....
....
....
....
....
....
....
....
....
....
....
....
....
....
....

Name them one by one.

Just before you start your day, as you're driving to school or sitting with your cup of morning something, write down one student's name. Then, as quickly as you can, write the positive distinct attributes of this student. Recall the times when he/she has surprised you; done well on an assignment; helped another; portrayed a good sense of humor; brought drama to an otherwise mundane scene; offered insight; prompted you to laugh out loud; and played his part well.

Hold this student in your heart and mind as you write or think these through. Then take a deep breath and see that student through these positive attributes. He/she doesn't ever need to know you have done this. The message will be carried by the intention and energy you have created. Cycle through your students in this fashion, until you come round to the first one again. It is a cycle of life that will be in the service of community.

....

....

....

....

....

....

....

....

....

....

....

....

....

....

....

....

....

....

The tail may be wagging the dog...

So, have you noticed that it seems school has become all about form? Fill this one out for the referral. Bring this one in by the end of the week, and don't forget to write it correctly. Recently, there has been a push for all teachers to be on the same page at the same time. All this in the name of "accountability."

To whom are we as teachers really accountable? The children are waiting for it to be them—that they are our first priority and that we come to school for their learning. But it can look and feel so different from that. If you must line up this way, must keep your voices down, and must align every lesson to standard-based assessment, what happens to the alignment of your soulful self and the spirit of learning?

Just because we began in the industrial age, as schools set out to be efficient in training the masses, doesn't mean we should remain there. We don't seem to be learning anything from even the academic and rigorous studies of how the brain learns, how long attention can be sustained, or how to keep neurological synapses firing.

We are ignoring so many larger truths about education for a smaller technical and mechanical way.

- We know that children learn best when they are curious, but we proceed to begin the lesson the same way, and it becomes predictable, not engaging.
- We have learned that there are at least nine forms of intelligence, but we just keep our focus on making students read and write.
- We believe that social and emotional intelligence is real and valid, but we succumb to the emphasis on *academics* most of the time.

We are shortchanging our lives as teachers and learners.

Set your intention for this day to become accountable to your students, holding what you know about learning to be your guide. Write below what comes to mind.

....

....

....

....

....

....

....

....

....

....

....

....

....

....

....

....

....

....

....

Call to circle

We learn from *Calling the Circle* by Christina Baldwin (1998) that when we gather in circle, the wisdom resides in the center. When we hear each voice round the circle, the intelligence expands and understanding deepens. The symbolic act of gathering in a circle conveys a nonhierarchical relationship, though one of the members may still hold the role of facilitator.

When I was in elementary school, our seats were in rows and actually bolted to the floor. I'm pretty sure this was for the convenience of the custodial staff. There were no circles, except on the playground when we would naturally cluster in our groups of chosen friends. Now, the chairs are moveable, so let us MOVE THEM. Let us see one another evenly. Let us sit together and feel our membership even for a few minutes a week. Call the circle and see what needs to be said, or ask a question...or just find out what's on their minds.

Write below one approach you might use for calling a circle in the next week.

Patty Lee, Ed. D.

....

....

....

....

....

....

....

....

....

....

....

....

....

....

....

....

....

....

You don't need a program for that!

These days, it seems we "fix" problems with programs. Got anger? We'll get you an anger management class. Been bullied? We'll set it straight by bully-proofing our schools. As if these human challenges could be solved by yet another curriculum in a box.

What do we honestly know about anger? Start there and notice the universal truths about it. Use these emotions of anger and mistreating one another as a natural occurrence that can be understood, that we all can share, and that each of us can speak about. And what "put-downs" are we all participating in? Why is it easy to bully? And what stories do the bullies have to tell?

Rather than another intervention, sometimes just a conversation about how these things happen is in order. Look inside yourself for this curriculum. Draw your wisdom from inner resources, from ancient wisdom. And keep the children as safe as you can.

Use the space below to write your own experience with anger and bullying. Notice where these stories live in you.

Where do you feel them? Let your own story serve as the teacher's manual.

....

....

....

....

....

....

....

....

....

....

....

....

....

....

Check it out inside.

It's so easy for a trend to develop where students in the classroom are tugging at our skirts and shirttails and asking us, "Is this okay, teacher?" "How long should it be?" "What are we supposed to do?" See me, hear me, and pay attention to me. And how do we feel in that energy? Crowded, exasperated—and, yes, often angry, just wanting it to go away.

So, how do we turn it around? Perhaps one way is to follow the advice of the author of *Spirit Whisperers* (2001), Chick Moorman, when he advised that teachers help develop student autonomy by inviting them to "check it out inside." This gives the students a chance to consult what they already know rather than to find out what the teacher wants. Other teachers have responded, "Ask three before me," so that students turn to one another first before going to the teacher.

It's easy for schools to encourage learner dependency, so that students are always looking to authority for the answer. As teachers, we have the power to break the cycle of dependency by changing our responses. What could your response be to students so that they will "check it out inside" first or rely more on their own resources? Brainstorm a few possibilities in the space below. Give it back to your students. They can handle it.

....

....

....

....

....

....

....

....

....

....

....

....

....

....

....

Every voice in the room

Sometimes we need to just hear from a few of our students. Sometimes we need to hear from everyone. As teachers, we've noticed that some students are eager to speak up while others are shy and keep their voices to themselves. It can be tempting to just call on the ones whose hands are raised and let the others be silent, but we know that's not what a learning community is about. So, we wonder how to draw out the quiet ones without putting them on the spot?

Perhaps it could happen this way. Designate different times you can specify as "Every Voice in the Room." When it is that time, ask a question that every child can answer in his/her own way. Every answer is the right one because it belongs to the responder. Possibilities include: What is your favorite food? What do you want to study next? What do you think about the work we just did? Where did your name come from? If you had another name, what would it be?

Listen closely to each answer without comment. This practice will encourage trust and community.

Use the space below to write examples of questions that do not have one right answer and can only be answered by the students individually. Then let every voice in the room respond.

....
....
....
....
....
....
....
....
....
....
....
....
....
....
....

What you need to know...

Throughout a teacher's career, she attends countless professional development workshops, and many are not of her own choosing. Systems are too often set up to tell teachers what they will learn and when.

You have some of the power in this situation. You simply decide. Think about something you are interested in learning more about, something you want to pursue further. Perhaps a lesson that you want to enhance with poetry or art. Or maybe you want to read a book like *Educating Esmé* by Esmé Codell and see how her adventures of her first year of teaching resonate with you.

Resources abound. There is most likely a colleague or two who would be great as a talking and thinking partner. What area would you like to explore? Maybe it's something about multiple intelligences, icebreakers, games that help in teaching your subject, interesting ways to start a lesson, or writing a limerick? Make this your own professional development.

Begin today. Ask a question that you truly want to answer. Write it below.

....

....

....

....

....

....

....

....

....

....

....

....

....

....

....

....

Perfection—give it up!

Have you noticed that your inner critic is on duty to the point of distraction? Do you nitpick at everything you attempt and rarely feel the satisfaction of "getting it right"? It may be that you are suffering from the disease of having to be perfect. Please, for the sake of yourself and your students, give it up! The world needs fewer perfectionists in general and especially fewer teachers who are trying to be perfect. Students pick up on your need for perfection in your life and think they have to have it in theirs.

It's as if they're saying to us:

When you have perfection as your destination, I feel less safe around you. When you only reward the perfectly done production, I don't want to hand mine in. When you make fun of a mistake I probably made, I am so ashamed. But you know, when you make fun of a mistake you made, I breathe differently, more deeply, and I laugh, too.

Let the students know you are still making mistakes, and they are a natural part of life. We've all heard that angels can fly because they take themselves lightly. Our schools could benefit from such wisdom. Lighten up! Use the space below to write your own commitment to embrace the mistakes in life and share them with your students.

....

....

....

....

....

....

....

....

....

....

....

....

It isn't fair...

When you let one student do something differently than another, you may hear something like, "It isn't fair that he gets to spell his words aloud when I have to write mine. It isn't fair that she gets to take a break when the rest of us are working. It isn't fair that you let her go to the board and not me. It just isn't fair."

Sound familiar? Kids are watching, and they are good at catching us when there is a discrepancy in the classroom. That's what our competitive society promotes. If I can catch you doing something wrong, I'll know your weakness and can use it to my benefit. As teachers, we can change this mentality, and, of course, we should begin with ourselves.

Ask yourself, "What is my definition of 'fairness'?" and "How does that apply in my classroom?" As facilitator of learning, you are the guide of how things are done and why. Let the students know that everyone learns differently; therefore, you may be asking for different ways of expressing what they know. This sets a tone of natural diversity and acceptance.

For too long, school has looked and felt like a place where everyone is expected to do the same thing and show their understanding in the same way. It takes courage, but you can mix it up a bit! If parents or administrators question your practice, let them know you are endeavoring to capitalize on each student's natural talents.

In the space below, draw an image or write a definition of your idea of fairness.

....

....

....

....

....

....

....

....

....

....

....

Do you know the teacher next door?

Donald Graves (2001) wrote *The Energy to Teach* by drawing from the answers to three questions that he asked hundreds of teachers:

1. What gives you energy?
2. What takes away energy?
3. What is just a plain waste of time?

As he reviewed the answers, he found that a key source of energy is the power of knowing one another—in our classrooms, in our schools. If you have just one colleague with whom you can talk and share ideas, you have a reservoir of energy from which to draw. Reaching out can help to address some of the isolation you may be feeling as a teacher. Knowing your next-door neighbor might just bring a lighter note to your day.

We tend to take ourselves very seriously in schools and may begin to compartmentalize our lives. Work/Play/Home. We don't talk about the movie we saw over the weekend; we simply close the door and take out the materials for the next lesson. Or our heart is breaking because of a recent loss, but we just keep going through the paces. Graves suggests that sometimes just the sharing of "how we are" with one another can open doors and energize this teaching life.

Take today and reach out, even for just a couple of minutes, and share something that might make them laugh, make them know what kind of movies you like, how a particular student just succeeded in something, or simply ask a REAL question that will help you know them better. It won't take long, and you'll both reap the benefits.

....

....

....

....

....

....

....

....

Please don't tell me anymore.

I used to go into her office to chat about various professional things we had in common. And then the conversation would turn to what I would call personal disdainful gossip about our colleagues. She would tell me something about another faculty member that was none of my business. When left with the information, I felt a little sick. How was I to respond to this recurring web of discomfort?

In the moment, I did not know what to say. I could only react inside and leave her presence as soon as possible. What response did I want to create? What could I say that would remove me from the trap I kept falling into? I didn't want to participate in this kind of exchange. It was up to me to change, because this was a pattern of hers that I thought she would continue. The more I just fell silent, the worse I felt.

So I began to practice things I might be able to say when situations like this occurred. Things like, "I'm really not comfortable knowing such things about_____"; or "You know, it makes me uneasy to talk this way about

_____." These did not come easily for me, and I would often rehearse in the privacy of my car on the way to work. But gradually, I was able to bring my own voice to the conversation and the result was a satisfying shift.

If you are currently experiencing something similar, feel free to use the space below to create your own possible responses. Staying true to oneself sometimes requires looking at your own patterns and revising them. As early as the 1500's, Sir Thomas More taught that *silence implies consent.*

....

....

....

....

....

....

....

....

....

....

No cell phones allowed.

We have our rules in schools. We know what is not allowed more than what is allowed, and we're sure right now that cell phones should not be allowed in schools. We don't want these bright shiny objects that all digital natives are drawn to competing with our student's attention. We still want it directed toward the front of the room...and guess who's there? The teacher who checks her cell phone between and sometimes during classes.

Anyway, it seems that we might use these devices better than just banning them. After all, isn't it logical that if we outlaw cell phones, only outlaws will have cell phones? If this all sounds a bit crazy making, it is. Let's see if we can approach this a different way. Let's ask students to show what they know by using their cell phones, tablets, or computers. Can we think intelligently enough to use the cell phone technology in an educational instructional way? Pose a question about the lesson. Maybe have them text their answers. Or have them write some of their vocabulary words the way they think they would be shortened in "text." Sure, I may be going way beyond the bounds right now, but I wouldn't have survived nor served as well as a teacher of fifty years had I stayed on the straight and narrow.

Technology is the water in which we swim these days. There are ways to make it work for us. Write some of those ways in the space below. Make it fun!

....

....

....

....

....

....

....

....

....

....

....

....

Who is intimidating you?

For me, it was a female colleague—a very tall, big woman whose size made me feel even shorter than my five-foot-three self. I don't know; just something about her made me feel less than I was. Less than I even knew myself to be. So I usually kept a low profile around her; I didn't speak about much of consequence. I guess you could say I was afraid of her.

Then one day, a student of hers came to me and asked that I be his college adviser instead of the tall woman. That request scared the hell out of me. What would she say? She would be so mad at me because *her* student wants to be under my advisement. But luckily, I simply asked the student why he desired that I be his advisor. He said, "Because you listen." It was a request that could not be denied. I told him to fill out the proper paperwork to get the change of advisor process started, and promptly began avoiding the female colleague.

Deep inside, I knew I was doing the right thing, but the ten-year-old in me was sure we would be in big trouble. I couldn't avoid her forever, and one day, she said, "We need to talk." She came into my office and expressed her disbelief that I would take a student from her; it was a big deal at the college level to have a certain number of doctoral students under your tutelage. In response, I said, "I'll bet you can't believe it; it would be hard for me, too, if the situation were reversed." I simply agreed with her. No defense, no explanation. My words kind of hung in the air, her posture softened, and we parted ways.

What a powerful thing to simply agree with the nature of her complaint! You may want to look around and get in touch with those people in your life whose presence make you feel less than your full self and see what your honest response might be.

....

....

....

....

....

....

What difference am I making, and how do I know?

This question is at the heart of reflective teaching. When we are reflective as teachers, we are learning from what we did, what effect we believe we had, and what we need to change to meet the needs of our students. Checking in with ourselves regularly offers a touchstone that can inform us of our actions and our efforts.

Donald Schön (1983), who has written extensively on the importance of reflection, has stated that, "Reflective practice is a 'dialogue' of thinking and doing through which I become more skillful." As a teacher, you are constantly reflecting, wondering why the lesson did not go as you planned and how you will change it next time, or how you can have them practice the skill yet another way.

But to ask yourself the question, "What difference am I making and how do I know?" is reflection at another level. It wakes us up to the path we were originally called to as teachers. It is important to record and live the answers to this question on a regular basis.

Maybe journaling is not for you; perhaps you'll draw images that represent your teaching and its effects. The poet in you may bring voice to this teaching journey. It's your story, and if you don't capture it along the way, it will be lost. No one else can tell your teaching story.

How might you begin this practice of reflection?

....

....

....

....

....

....

....

....

....

....

....

....

....

....

I don't get it.

Too often, we are assuming that students understand when indeed they don't. We move on; the pace is quick; we have much to do. But do they understand the instructions? The concept? The sequence of content? Maybe you can build a new repertoire of ways to find out what they understand in your class.

Think about the nature of understanding. When we understand something, we can usually explain it to another. So, rather than you as teacher always being the one who clarifies, open it up to the students and witness their understanding as they share it with each other. Have it become the norm in your classroom that confusion is natural and sits right at the edge of learning.

Maybe you can stop from time to time and check the understanding in the room. Have the students share what they understood from the lesson with a neighbor. Ask a couple of sets of partners to explain what they have just learned or understood. We are wasting their time and ours if, in our haste to "cover" the content, we are not checking for their perspectives and understanding.

Write below a few ways you can use to check for understanding in your classroom. When you practice these, I think you'll be surprised at the range of understanding among your students, and you'll have an idea of who and what might need a bit more or less attention.

....

....

....

....

....

....

....

....

....

....

....

Finding the artist in you...

This craft of teaching is yours to find and develop. It is the next book you read that excites you about its message, making you want to bring it into your classroom. It's the idea that wakes you up in the middle of the night or comes to you in a dream meant to manifest between you and your students. It's a painting you've seen that draws you in; it's your right brain leading the way. It's why you entered this profession in the first place—to be so excited by that spark and flash of learning that you must give it away.

So many are quick to say, "I'm not an artist," and too many think art is a place you go to down the hall, and you make art in that room only. That's how school has looked for too long, and you can help us change that. Beginning with ourselves, we consider who is the artist within? Notice what art expressions take your breath away, make you want to look more closely, or sit quietly and just take it in.

Maybe you'll get out your colored pencils and join the students for a five-minute sketching activity, with everyone noticing and naming their favorite colors and designs. Or perhaps you'll put on a piece of music that always brings you peace and calm, watching how it effects your classroom environment.

Take the space below to image your artistic ways: things you love to create, gardens you have planted, colors you delight in, patterns that make you smile. See how you can imbed them in your teaching life.

....

....

....

....

....

....

....

....

....

....

....

....

Parents are people, too.

We all know about programs to increase parent involvement, and we know too well the phrase, "the parents who really needed to be here were not." While we are here to invite and draw the parents into their child's education; it does us little good to continue to judge some as good or bad depending on our perspective of how they support their child.

It's as if we have come to treat parents as a separate entity and something to be contended with, often polarizing our efforts and creating an "us vs. them" mentality. That is not good for our health nor the health of our planet, and we can shift this relationship with parents by some very simple means.

Let's take parent conferences. The models we have created for parent conferences are far more about the convenience of the system than for human interaction. Some schools schedule the conferences every fifteen minutes, with little or no breaks in between. So, while the teacher has maybe ten to twelve conferences in a row, the parent just has ONE of those. They come with apprehension to find out how their student is doing. They come with their own past relationship with school, what it meant to them, and the comfort or discomfort they felt. And they come with their hearts on their sleeves, for this is their lifeblood we're talking about here. Maybe one authentic open-ended question could serve us better and get us acquainted differently.

"How would you describe this school year for your child?" or "What do you believe his/her number one need is?"

You don't have to *meet* every need. You simply want to convey that this parent knows things about their child that you can never know, that their perspective is important to you. Parents are first people, and we happen to share their children for a brief period of time.

Write below some possible questions with which you might open a parent conference. Think of what you would like *your* child's teacher to ask you at a parent conference. Perhaps you can begin a new and different conversation.

....

....

....

....

....

....

....

....

....

....

....

....

....

....

....

....

....

....

....

She kept a stone in the crook of a tree.

We were sitting in a circle of teachers identifying the things that had become touchstones in our lives. One teacher, who taught at Tesuque Elementary in New Mexico, told us of her touchstone. She kept it in the crook of a tree just off the playground. She could get to it easily at recess or break, and, most of all, she knew it was there. This stone was her reminder of the bigger world, the natural world, the ancient knowing that we too easily forget. This stone reminded her of something older and wiser than herself. It was one of her spirit guides that represented why she was here, where she was, and that the children in her class were of a large and natural world.

I'm sure you have touchstones of all kinds in your life, and I'm suggesting that selecting a specific touchstone for your teaching life can serve you, especially in crazy times. Choose a particular object that has meaning for you that you can carry in your pocket, put in your desk at school, or place in a secret place like the crook of a tree. Maybe it will be one that reminds you of why you wanted to teach in the first place. Perhaps it will calm you and help you center yourself rather than get caught up in the drama of the moment.

Consider the possibilities of touchstones that would work for you, and write them here.

....

....

....

....

....

....

....

....

....

....

....

....

....

....

Try it with your non-dominant hand

Want to feel less than competent? Just write a while with your non-dominant hand. Use the space below and write your name and address. How did that feel? A little vulnerable? Good. That may be how our students are feeling toward many of our assignments. We are putting them in a tenuous position, wondering if they can do what we've asked, unable to read what they've just written, unsure of how they'll measure up. For those of us who teach, it is good practice to experience the vulnerability in ourselves from time to time; otherwise, we get in a space of false security and surety. We may come across as though we are competent in everything, yet we know that's not the case. If we want students to know it's all right to struggle, all right to practice, all right to speak softly at first, we must keep our own moments of learning close at hand.

When we touch that shy and less-than-competent part of ourselves, we come alive differently. Think back to when you were their age. What were you unsure of? What frightened or embarrassed you in school? Notice where you feel this in your body. Bring that awareness to your classroom. Let it be your guide; it will help you walk in their shoes.

....

....

....

....

....

....

....

....

....

....

....

....

....

....

....

....

Why do they keep leaving?

You probably know some of them—teachers who thought that school was where they wanted to be yet leaving the profession after three to four years; students graduating from teacher education programs with stars in their eyes and a pulse of idealism beating in their veins. They indeed believed they could change the world, and school was the place they wanted to make that change. But it isn't always working out that way, and idealism in the face of reality in the public schools can wear a teacher's soul down quickly and sometimes brutally.

Under the same conditions, others stay. Some become master teachers and wouldn't want to be doing anything else.

And what about you on this course? I hope you are finding the resources that support your teaching path and help you make sense of the sometimes seemingly senseless ways of school. The resources that support teachers are both internal and external. Pay careful attention to those really good days and ponder what came into play to make it such a positive experience on your drive home. Savor it a while.

Angeles Arrien (1993) cautions us against the habit of paying more attention to the "whispers of self-diminishment" than to the sweet acknowledgement of a job well done.

Staying the course in this profession means finding yourself over and over in a place called school. You'll be learning from the bumps in the road, picking yourself up and brushing yourself off, just as you want your students to be able to do.

You may want to write below a timeline of your teaching life thus far. Put the positive years, months, or weeks above the line and the difficult ones below the line. See what this tells you, and think about what it might tell you a year from now.

....

....

....

....

....

....

What story are you telling?

Do your students know you as a storyteller? I'm sure you know about those times you start to tell them a story, and they seem to pay attention differently. They lean forward a bit; they appear to be listening more intently. They're curious. They want to know your story—that you have been a child, that you have cried, that you still are learning, and that your story is no better, no bigger than theirs.

Storytelling is strikingly different than giving information; it makes information come alive. There is a palpable difference of telling someone not to go near the river, because they could drown, they could get hurt, and on and on, versus telling them the nature of the river and how it behaves. When you tell about the river in story, you note where it comes from, why it is important, and what power it possesses, and maybe what it does with things in its path. This brings a different and respectful understanding of the river.

So, my question is this: What can you touch in yourself that invites the storyteller to your classroom? Remember a turning point in your life after which you were never the same. Think about something that happened to you that you would have never chosen, but it made all the difference in your life, or a time you took a risk and were scared to death, but you DID IT!

Find these stories, give them life again and tell them. They are yours to give away. Your stories are the students' stories. Ponder the possibilities below.

....

....

....

....

....

....

....

....

....

....

....

Can I doodle in class?

I was teaching at UNC in a graduate course when a student came to me after class and asked me, "Do you mind if I knit in class?" To tell you the truth, I was a bit offended, as I was far more comfortable with students who nodded their heads and took notes in my classroom. It made me think they were actually attending to the topic and what I said.

By the grace of some intelligent spirit, I asked her why she wanted to knit during class. She answered simply, " I learn better when my hands are busy." I had to ask myself the next question: *What teacher would deny a student learning better in her class?* So, of course, my response was, "Yes, you may." She proceeded to knit every class from then on, finishing a nice afghan by the end of the semester.

Thank goodness I allowed this differentiated learning in my classroom even before I knew what to call it. Oh, I was a bit skeptical about what the other students would say, and what my peers might think when I let someone knit in my class, but I stayed in touch with the deepest truth. I wanted students to learn in this class, and if knitting was helpful to this student and not too distracting to others, my question was: why not? I almost got trapped by fearing what others would say, but I simply kept true to what I knew was the right thing to do.

Much of our schooling is set up around convenience to the adults. Maybe your students want to doodle, color, close their eyes, sit somewhere else, or listen to music as they work. The question you might pose to yourself is: will it significantly disrupt the others or the learning environment? See if it isn't possible to allow for more individual choice in your classroom. Jot down some possibilities that come to mind.

....

....

....

....

....

....

....

Remember the power you have

How we are treated by our teachers lives in us for a long time, sometimes forever. Maybe one of your teachers treated you in a way you will never forget. Good, bad, and yes, even ugly. My friend remembers a time in fourth grade where the normal routine was to take turns reading aloud around the room. When it came her turn, the teacher called her to the front of the class and stood over her, reading aloud *for* her in a most condescending manner. It makes you wonder if the teacher thought that my friend could be shamed into reading better. This situation was so blatantly demeaning, abusive, and heartbreaking, and it lives deeply in my friend as an adult.

Other examples are subtler. It can be just a look of disgust, rolling of eyes in a particular way, or tone of voice when the day has gotten on the last nerve you have. Just remember that the power you have as a teacher is astounding, and who you are will live in your students in ways you cannot imagine.

In the space below, write the first memories of how you were treated by teachers—good, bad, and ugly. That is part of their legacy. What do you want yours to be?

....

....

....

....

....

....

....

....

....

....

....

....

....

....

....

Seductions to be less than you are.

Do you know how it is to avoid the teacher's lounge or workroom because you don't want to hear all the negativity? You go in to eat your lunch, and you end up eating something toxic that was not meant to be part of your meal. You cannot help but eat it, and it probably is not great for your digestion.

There is a victim mentality living in too many schools— even among teachers. The cynicism of "it's just the administration taking advantage of us again," "there's nothing we can do about it," or "the parents are really to blame because they don't see to it that students do their homework, yada, yada, yada." A victim mentality will never lift you to your higher self. It will not help you step back and take a breath and see the forest for the trees. It will instead take you to a darker place of "I can't make a difference"...and that's just not true.

If you put your energy into trying to change the system— the people around you, the parents, or the administrators— your cynicism will grow and you will feel increasingly out of control. Instead, take the step to change your response and avoid the cynicism. Your ability to stay clear in being the role model your students are counting on will guide you to a better place and energy. Describe below any situations where you feel you are getting caught in being less than you know you are.

....

....

....

....

....

....

....

....

....

....

....

....

Seeing distinctly, Seeing each one.

I facilitated a book study with teachers last year around the topic of mindfulness. One of the activities in our book, *"Mindful Teaching and Teaching Mindfulness,"* (2009) was about mindful seeing. It suggests that you find or make a collection of things that look very similar but are individually distinct. I chose some small red jasper rocks. As the basket was passed around, each teacher took one rock and kept it in her hand. Then I asked that they look at the rock carefully on all sides, so that when it was returned to the collection, it could be recognized for its own individual attributes. They studied the rocks for two to three minutes, turning them over and taking in the nuances. Then the basket was passed around, and each person put their own rock back in the group. After a bit, the basket was passed around the circle again, and each teacher reclaimed her own rock. They had "seen" the rocks for the individual characteristics and not just its similarity to all the others. It had become theirs to claim...and they were pleased.

One of the teachers took this activity to her art class as she introduced a lesson. The kids were fascinated to look closely at the rocks, study the uniqueness of their own, and reclaim it without question. She reported that the students were much more focused than usual throughout the remainder of the class. It was so much more powerful than other ways she had been using to get their attention. They were "seeing" differently. Consider below some possible ways to prompt mindful hearing and seeing within your students.

....

....

....

....

....

....

....

....

....

Reactive—Creative

For quite some time, I've mused over the fact that these two words are anagrams—having all the same letters, and meaning very different things when rearranged. Being one of these often precludes the ability to be the other. When I am just reacting to things, my creativity is usually not in play. And what does that mean for you, dear teacher? When our reactive selves are in charge, our creative selves can lie dormant, undeveloped, and out of reach. As you want the students in your classes to be creative, so I wish the same for you.

What can you do to shift the power? Well, let's start with where you feel the most creative and what you love to do. Piano, poetry, origami, knitting, walking in the woods under a full moon, painting your walls, painting a picture. Get back in touch with the creative expressions that bring you delight. Don't put them off until summer break. Your students need these creative juices in the classroom. Grab a minute and make it yours. Once in a while, ask the students to paint or draw their understanding of a lesson they've completed, or tap out a rhythm of the next math problem.

In the space below, use some colored pens and draw a map of your creative joys. Which one will you take to school today?

....

....

....

....

....

....

....

....

....

....

....

....

....

....

....

How many mistakes does it take?

After exploring how to develop a viable electric light bulb for months and months, Thomas Edison was interviewed by a young reporter who boldly asked him if he felt like a failure and if he thought he should just give up by now. Perplexed, Edison replied, "Young man, why would I feel like a failure? And why would I ever give up? I now know definitively over 9,000 ways that an electric light bulb will not work. Success is almost in my grasp." Shortly after that, and over 10,000 attempts, Edison invented the light bulb.

According to Edison, when working to create filament, it took many mistakes, and each of them important, each of them getting him closer to a divine truth that would change our world. Yet, in schools, we often equate mistakes with something distasteful. I spoke to a dear friend recently who told me that when she handed her paper into her fifth grade teacher, it was returned with red marks all over it, and it was all about what was wrong. By the way she told the story, it is still a painful memory, and one that affected her subsequent performance in school.

Now as an adult, she holds that as central to her own story of school. Can you help us change that for your students? Let the students know what they have done well, and then give them guidance about the mistakes they have made, instead of just marking them wrong.

If we can make this shift, we can truly change how students view their own work and help them know how to go about improving. In the space below, brainstorm your own ideas for demonstrating, modeling, embodying, and evidencing that, in your classroom, mistakes are to be embraced, for they are our greatest teachers.

....

....

....

....

....

....

....

....

I carry his picture with me.

One of the teachers in my college class told us of a practice she does annually. She has individual photos of all of her students, and when the year is ending, she spreads them all out and looks at their faces. Then she selects one photo of a student she thinks she didn't reach that year. It wasn't that she failed; it's something greater than that. It's about the teaching practice she is developing. She carries that photo with her through the summer as she takes her own respite from the school year. It gives her pause, focus, and humility, setting her on her course for the future.

Of course, this could be done several times a year, and with variations of what it represents in your teaching practice. When you have individual photos of each student before you, it heightens your awareness of them, their lives, and your relationship to them.

So, take out your phone or dust off that camera and take some photos of your students as part of a regular school day. Then keep the pictures someplace you can see them often, and ask for the guidance you need in reaching as many of them as possible.

....

....

....

....

....

....

....

....

....

....

....

....

....

....

....

Living your legacy now.

As a teacher, what do you want to be remembered for? This question is central to your call to teach and the legacy you want to leave. I'm sure there are aspirations you have as a teacher, as well as values that you long to convey. These core beliefs may be central to your life, and you want to pass them along.

At a summer institute for teachers, participants were asked to remember a teacher who had left a significant impression on them and to describe what they remembered about that teacher. Many times, the responses were something like, "She saw me," "She knew I could do better and believed in me," "He wore costumes to get his point across," or "He kept asking me questions that made me more curious." After these experiences were shared in the institute, the teachers wrote a letter to their students about the teacher they were striving to be and how they wanted to bring that forward into the new school year. They were attending to legacy.

So here's a little activity to get you in touch with your purpose and therefore your desired legacy. Take a minute to complete the sentence below:

"I came into this profession to_____ so that _____."

After you've completed the sentence, write your own thoughts about whether the path you are currently on as a teacher will lead to the outcome you have expressed in the unfinished sentence. Maybe something needs to shift a bit, or perhaps you are on course. What do you think your students will remember you for this year?

....

....

....

....

....

....

....

....

Everyone needs special education...

When I began studying special education in the area of learning disabilities, I was thrilled to have the focus of considering one learner at a time. After years of serving children in large groups, I was at last able to look at the capabilities of the child and help build a program that would develop and sustain them. To sit with parents and help them dream and imagine the future that could be attained by their son or daughter was an honor and a privilege.

And then I watched the form of it all take over—the compliance with the law and the boxes that needed to be checked took precedence over co-creating an educational plan for each child. Special education, which was intended to be a comprehensive way of seeing and serving each child individually, had become a paper-laden process that often lost sight of the original intention. I'm afraid that we have become more successful at filling in the forms for special education than in creatively meeting the needs of individuals with different learning challenges.

As teachers, perhaps you can help us get back the original spirit of special education. Maybe before the next Individualized Education Planning meeting that you are required to attend, you can give the parent a call and ask a few questions related to what they hope for their child, how they feel this year in school is going, or what they'd specifically like to hear about their child's progress. It is *you* who can bring meaning to this meeting by simply making a human connection. In advocating for this child, you can join the parent in bringing a bit of their agenda to the table.

Consider below how this devolution of special education is true at your school and what you can do to help humanize a cold and overly businesslike process. Just because it's bound by law doesn't mean we have to eliminate the personal touch.

....

....

....

....

....

....

Wondering...

Somewhere around 1995, Maxine Greene, Professor Emeritus at Teachers College, was sitting at the front of the room as a presenter in a national education conference session that I attended. She was musing on the changes brought about by technology of the day. She couldn't believe that typing on a keyboard would ever be as sacred as scratching it out in pencil or pen on a yellow legal pad. And, as we moved closer to No Child Left Behind legislation, she spoke to a simple truth that reassured me about my own core values. With all the focus on measurement, SMART goals, and behavioral trends, she simply stated that there should be one primary standard for graduation from high school.

That assessment standard for graduation should be:

What are you still wondering? What are you curious about? What do you want to figure out? What difference might that make?

To wonder is to engage your own curiosity, to ask the next question, to ponder what-if, and to dream of what might be. To wonder is to marvel; it is a precious living thing, this wonder we are able to do.

You might ask yourself, "What am I wondering about these days? What is intriguing to me?" Maybe you're wondering about how origami is done. Perhaps you're curious if weather is actually predictable or if the color lavender might enhance your home. Take that wonder into your day and see what "news" it elicits. Write below something you are wondering about. Share it with your students and see what they're wondering. Such a laudable pastime. ☺

....

....

....

....

....

....

I thought it was just me...

How many teachers feel utterly alone? And I'm wondering about you. How are you doing in this profession that keeps teachers from one another? It is especially common for new teachers to feel quite isolated, not having the time nor thinking partners to process the daily happenings. Parker Palmer (1998) has advocated "teachers talking with teachers about teaching" as one of the most critical missing links in our profession.

There is a tonic for this aloneness. When teachers sit in community circles and share their stories, more often than not, several will say that they thought they were the only one who was feeling that way (i.e., overwhelmed, like it's become a game, unappreciated, unacknowledged, put upon, etc.).

When they hear the commonality of these themes, there is a relief, a release, and recognition of the human ties that bind. Once released, these teachers can move on to what is next for them—to grow themselves and to practice their craft with renewed courage, because they have found their kin.

They are a part of something larger than their own classrooms. They are teachers who care deeply about themselves, their students, and one another. We simply need more teachers sharing this way with one another.

Consider below your own experience with aloneness and that of collegial community. Many teachers are feeling the way you feel. Is there one you want to reach out to?

....

....

....

....

....

....

....

....

....

....

....

It's in your circle...

Stephen Covey, in *Seven Habits of Highly Effective People* (1989), teaches that we live in two circles: our circle of concern and our circle of influence.

Circle of Concern

For teachers, the circle of concern contains all of the things we feel helpless to change yet are affecting learning: the home environment of our students, the violent neighborhoods in which they live, the new mandate from central office, the lack of materials in our classrooms, or the number of students that make up our classes. As an individual teacher, we know the impact of these conditions, yet we feel powerless in affecting change.

Circle of Influence

On the other hand, our circle of influence is the place where what we do has a good chance of making a difference: how we listen to the next child; the breath we take before we say something in disgust; what we learn new about a student that expands our appreciation; what questions we ask to draw a student out; how often we bring humor to our classrooms; how we are playful in school; or how well we've planned our lesson with students and learning in mind.

When we *spend* our energy only in the circle of concern, we exhaust ourselves by worry and blame. When we *invest* our energy in our circle of influence, we have a chance to get a return on that investment, and there is less chance of burning out.

Draw the two circles below. Label the aspects that often whirl around in your circle of concern. Then name the things that exist in your circle of influence. Give your attention to one of those today, and do your best to "let go" of the things you cannot control.

Watch out for next year's class.

Can you believe it? Because we educate the students in masses, they almost become that in our reaction to them. You hear about a class that's coming to you the next year, how they are troublemakers, and how the teacher before you had the worst year ever with them. And, indeed, there may be a seed of truth in what you hear. Every classroom has its dynamic, and some are far more challenging than others, challenging the teacher you so want to become.

And what do **you** have each year no matter which students arrive? You have your own core strength of beliefs and values in what learning is all about. This strength serves you on good and bad days. It's like muscles that must be trained, exercised, and developed. It isn't always there in the same amount, and it can be weakened when resistance is too great.

You must tend to your teaching spirit by checking in and tuning in, so that the kids reap the benefit of a mentor who is not getting swept away by the drama of other people. What is the core value that needs to be strengthened in you right now?—patience, flexibility, gratitude, perseverance, or alignment? Working toward your own sustainability as teacher will build a lifelong resource. Maybe these "difficult" kids are just the next level of your fitness program.

Your thoughts...

....

....

....

....

....

....

....

....

....

....

....

....

....

....

Who is an artist? Who can dance?

When we ask children in early childhood if they can draw, dance, or sing, they are quick to not only say *yes* but to show us indeed how they are artists, poets, and dancers. Then a couple of years later, when we ask them the same questions, many of them are not so sure...maybe they can draw...nope, they definitely cannot dance. They have become shy to sing for you.

And teacher friend, how about you? Weren't you once an artist, singer, and dancer? Do you recall when you last painted a picture? Have your students known this side of you? Kids love when teachers open up to the artistic expression inside of them. It makes for a whole different learning environment. Everyone feels safer to explore, be silly, and have fun with colors, images, ideas and unique expressions.

It's time to find more ways to sing and dance in our classrooms. We need more chances to inspire the artists inside. Maybe you could take a favorite picture off your wall at home and take it to school with you. Put it in a prominent place, but do not say anything about it. Wait until the questions come, because they will. After talking about it, have the students take out three colors and a piece of paper, large or small. Ask them to draw something it reminds them of; write a poem about what they see; or dramatize the kind of person who might have created such a picture. Mix it up briefly with the academic pool you're swimming in. The right brains of the children will be grateful. ☺

....

....

....

....

....

....

....

....

....

....

Why must you sink for me to swim?

We are so highly competitive in this culture. It is the water in which we swim. It is the air we breathe. It is why children cheat. Why do they not trust their own answers? Why do they resist checking out what they know and instead look across to what a neighbor has answered? As teachers, we need to ask ourselves: *What am I doing in my classroom that perpetuates this competitive energy?*

When I read *The Case Against Competition* by Alfie Kohn (1987), I found a philosophy that resonated strongly with me—one that I wanted to practice in my classroom. I wasn't sure just how I would bring such a notion into a school where everything was compared, high scores were revered, and competition and athletics reigned supreme. But I wanted to try. I knew we were losing something significant by emphasizing an *"I-swim-you-sink"* mentality.

So, I examined my own teaching and expectations and asked myself how I might change any of that. Could I make grades less important and still meet the requirements of the district? Where was I reinforcing one student's work over another? Most of all, how were students gauging their own progress? I decided I could change one small thing, and that is often what's needed when we take on something new. I decided to have the students learn to evaluate their own and one another's work. I didn't need to be the sole grade giver. This could make the rubrics we were using even more valuable and meaningful.

As teachers, we need to reflect on how we are emphasizing the competitive aspect of student performance and see what we can do to keep from pitting one against another.

I also learned I could ask better questions after sports events, which would engage the students differently. I began to ask things like, "What was the hardest part of the game?" "How would you play differently next time?" "Would you consider this game/event a really difficult one or fairly easy?" "What are you working to improve in your game?" These served for far more interesting conversations than "Who won?"

Use the space below to write your own ideas and beliefs about competition.

....

....

....

....

....

....

....

....

....

....

....

....

....

....

....

....

....

....

Not who you really are.

A fifth-grade teacher in Santa Fe was deeply concerned with the behavior of one of her students. The frequent disruptions in the classroom distracted everyone. So, one day, after an outburst, the teacher caught up with the student on the playground and began to walk beside her. She simply said to the student, "You know those things you did in the classroom? Those things I asked you to stop doing? Those things that were disrupting? Well, I don't happen to believe that's who you really are. You may be frustrated, angry, overwhelmed, but I think you are more than that. I think you are caring, have a great sense of humor, and maybe just wanted some attention. I'm hoping that this year in fifth grade, we'll have a chance to know the *real* you."

We ARE more than our behaviors, but in our institutions, the behaviors sometimes get the attention. And if they are not in line with the institution, they are punished and restricted in some way. Maybe it's time to find your way to say to some of your students, "I don't think that's who you really are."

In the space below, name the students who come to mind when you read the words, "I don't think that's who you really are."

....

....

....

....

....

....

....

....

....

....

....

....

....

....

What are you learning?

Do the students know that you are still learning? Or do they think you're all done with that? ☺ You've figured everything out. You have answers for it all. Too many times in our schools, teachers come across as having it all together and knowing just what they're up to.

If we want students to be engaged learners, we need to model some of that ourselves. Maybe you've gone to a workshop or class recently and learned a new teaching strategy. Perhaps you found out something in the news that you had no idea about. Or you were stunned to learn something about a friend whom you thought you knew pretty well. If you can share these incidences with your students, they will have the chance to know you are still learning, and it never ends.

One of the displays in your classroom could be *What We're Learning*, where everyone, including you, puts a sticky note now and then about something they learned recently. In classrooms, we want to convey we are in this together, and learning is something everyone is doing. When

I know that my teacher is still learning, I have more trust in my own learning.

Consider other ways that come to mind about sharing your own learning with your students.

....

....

....

....

....

....

....

....

....

....

....

....

....

....

....

Are you WITH them?

As teachers, it's often easier to be separated from your students than to be with them; to feel as though you have something to COVER and no time to uncover, or discover; to rush through the lessons because that is what is on the schedule; or to lose touch with the natural rhythm of learning and push things into a predetermined form and schedule.

Perhaps today can be different, or just ten minutes of today can be different. Maybe you can sit with them and not stand before them. Maybe you can go deeply into just one aspect of the lesson at hand and talk about what you're curious about, asking them the same. Or, more radically, when they are writing in their journals, you could, too!

I can promise you this: if you are able to be *with* them just once in a while, you will find respite. Jot down ways that convey you are *WITH* your students.

Leap of faith...

I was teaching a class in collaboration in the Department of Special Education. There were only nine in my class, one of the gifts of graduate school. We had made a consensual decision to write a book. Each person in the class would write a chapter, and we would edit it as a group; thus, learning about each other's chapter content and going in depth with the one we authored. Midway through the class, one of the students, Janet, came to me and told me she knew nothing about special education and wanted to contribute something different to our class. I asked her what her background was, and she replied, "I'm a dancer."

Though I went totally blank, I simply said to her, "Let me think about it, and we'll talk next week."

The week passed and I had not thought about it at all; luckily, she had. Before class that evening, she came to me and asked what I had decided. From an unrecognizable source, I heard myself asking, "How would you like to *dance* your understanding of our class in collaboration?" WHAT HAD I JUST SAID? How could that be?

Before my anxiety became full blown, she calmed me down by answering, "Could I really do that?"

And I thought, "If you can *do* that, then yes, you *can* do that."

The next to the last night of class, Janet came adorned in full dance regalia and carrying her boom box. Before she turned on the music, she explained to us that she was going to "dance her understanding" of collaboration and consultation between regular and special education. A new energy filled that classroom, as Janet was able to speak in her language and not just conform to ours.

How can we follow our students' lead? How can we say "yes" where the system has been saying "no, not here"? Take this question into your day and listen to what the students are telling you. It's worth the risk.

....

....

....

....

....

You push my buttons

There are people who will really push your buttons, and because kids are people, they are capable of doing the same. So it's good to know where your buttons are, and who is particularly adept at pushing them. Maybe it's the kid who rolls his eyes at you, maybe the one who constantly picks on other kids, maybe the one who cannot quit talking, interrupting, and generally calling attention to himself. It just seems when that child behaves in that way, it gets to you more quickly and offends you more deeply. Typically, you react—internally at least and sometimes externally in ways you regret.

Well, guess what? The buttons are inside you, developed by you, and perpetuated by you. So guess what else? You get to reprogram them. Not easy but surely possible. Write below the names of a few students who "push your buttons". Then go back to each name and write alongside a short description of that button and the reaction it prompts in you. Can you bring a light to one of these and write a new response that could break the cycle? Maybe it's a softening.

Maybe it's a smile. Maybe you "see" it turn to vapor in the wind. Maybe you just simply ignore something that has always triggered you before.

This human endeavor of teaching and learning is indeed humbling.

....

....

....

....

....

....

....

....

....

....

....

....

....

....

I used to think...and now I think

Richard Elmore (2011), who has edited a book in the area of education reform, asked teachers of all levels and tenure to reflect on the prompt "*I used to think, and now I think...*" This line of investigation leads us to understand where we've been, how things have shifted for us, and where we might be going as a result. It helps students open up to ways they are changing, and could be the topic for a whole unit where family members are interviewed and photos are shared representing "used to" and "now". Or it could be the topic of a faculty meeting. Teachers would learn a lot from each other's reflections on these prompts.

This inquiry can open rich dialogue and reveal new insights. You may want to shift the inquiry: I used to believe, and now I believe. I used to feel, and now I feel. I used to dream, and now I dream. I used to want, and now I want. I used to need, and now I need. The possibilities end at the edge of your imagination.

Have fun with it!

....

....

....

....

....

....

....

....

....

....

....

....

....

....

....

....

....

....

Do you hear your own voice?

What voice are you developing as a teacher? As a human being? What do you hear yourself saying? What tone do others hear when they listen to you? Do you recognize it as your own voice or that of someone else? When does your voice least belong to you? When do you feel the most vulnerable in expressing yourself?

For me, it was in faculty meetings with my peers. If I spoke, my neck turned red, and I felt the voice was outside me, certainly not embodied. It's really something to say what you feel or believe in the presence of one's colleagues, especially where voicing our opinions may not be the norm. It seems even harder when you have an opinion that has not been expressed. This is a risk many teachers are not willing to take. They are afraid to state a truth that might offend, and so they remain silent. You may know the feeling of strongly disagreeing with a new plan or curriculum that's being implemented, but you do not speak up. It seems easier to remain silent and maybe later speak to another colleague you can trust.

I believe we are all missing out by not expressing our opinions. Teachers need to hear one another. As a profession too isolated and shrouded in silence, teachers need to experience honest collegial conversation. Because we are more alike than different, when we express our true thoughts, it clears the way for others to share their stories, which is at the center of creating community. Parker Palmer (2010) believes that the health and democracy of schools depends upon teachers talking to one another about good teaching, whether we agree or disagree.

Use the space below to consider your developing voice. How do you believe you are coming across? Is there something you wish to express but haven't found the words? Write about it here.

....

....

....

....

....

....

Why are you screaming at her?

It was the first day of kindergarten, and there were twenty-six new students. Some came with deer-in-the-headlights look; others were expressing eager curiosity. Some were crying quietly in the corner, and one was howling! Several moms had asked to stay at school with their children on this first day, and the teacher obliged but asked them to sit just outside the classroom door. That way the children would know they were there, but the teacher could begin to establish a community in the classroom.

Suddenly, the principal arrived and came into the room and began yelling at the teacher. "Your classroom is out of control!" Got the picture? Feel the absurdity? Now, we have adults yelling at adults about not being able to quiet the five-year-olds.

It's easy for us to slip into being louder than we mean to and sounding harsher than we intend to as we work to get the attention of 20+ students. But we owe it to the students in our charge to continue to model and practice the way we want them to become—to speak in respectful tones and find ways that honor the energy in the classroom, as well as encourage collaboration.

Students will always learn more deeply from what we do than what we say, so consider taking a look at that today. What are our children seeing in teachers? What do you want them to see in you? How can you BE that? Jot your thoughts below.

....

....

....

....

....

....

....

....

....

....

....

....

You are here at just the right time.

Many days with many students—it may seem you have landed in a place of chaos and overwhelm. The common core standards are breathing down your neck; the external expectations swallow your own internal knowing and belief in yourself and sometimes in the entire profession.

But you are here now, and the students in front of you are the ones you're meant to have. They are in your charge. The external demands have always been there. They come and go like weather. They wear different colors and come with a variety of names, but they are not permanent. The students are the constant that matters; their learning is your true calling.

Take a moment and write down all of the external demands that are pulling and tugging at your sanity. Write them as quickly as you can, and then one by one, loosen the tie that binds them to you. Unravel some of them completely. You are in control of your own response to these. The unraveling will free your energy and give you space for learning.

What are those ties that are binding right now?

....

....

....

....

....

....

....

....

....

....

....

....

....

....

....

....

....

....

Student of the month

You cannot think of every student every day, but you can hold one student in your focus each day. And if you make that a practice, you will hold that student in your thoughts every twenty to twenty-five days instead of trying to hold them all every day.

This idea was given to me long ago when I was working in a program of students with disabilities and going crazy trying to think about each of the eighteen staff members every day. My therapist ☺ suggested that I pay special attention to *one* staff member a day—checking in with them, asking them a personal question, mentioning something you know is important to them. It was a mindfulness practice, attending to one person even for five minutes that day in a way I would never have when trying to hold all of them all of the time.

My suggestion is that you try this with your students. They are waiting to be seen, to be asked a question that only they can answer, to get to tell you how their family is, what they named their puppy, or what helps them most in school.

Patty Lee, Ed. D.

Set up your calendar days with their individual names and find out how and who they are. I think you'll be pleased with the connections you make and the focus it brings.

....

....

....

....

....

....

....

....

....

....

....

....

....

....

....

....

....

Slow down! You move too fast...

School schedules wear me out! How about you? The nonstop pace is sucking the life out of all of us. We're living in a model that is artificial and often has little to do with the organic nature of learning. We've divided this subject from that, this time period equal to that, and it's depleting us all of the natural rhythms we have.

There are remedies for this epidemic. Take a walk slowly and notice what you notice. Stop and take a closer look. Is that water you hear running? How thankful are you for water? Might there be a way you can bring that timelessness into your classroom space even for a few moments? Close your eyes for just a bit and guess how many seconds have passed. Try that with your students. Ask them to move in slow motion from one activity to another. Elementary students especially love to do this. A high school teacher slowed things down a bit by beginning each class with a soft bell. Ask students to take three deep breaths before you change an activity. Listen to yourself. Are you talking at breakneck speed?

Consider ways you can slow down in your classroom even for a couple of minutes today.

....

....

....

....

....

....

....

....

....

....

....

....

....

....

....

It matters not how smart you are, but HOW you are smart.

Howard Gardner (1983) was curious about the nature of intelligence and began a phenomenal exploration of how people come to learn, know, and master a particular area. His theory of multiple intelligences is broad and deep, and has caused many a teacher to say, "Yes, yes, we know this is so." His work has uplifted the areas of spatial, musical, kinesthetic, interpersonal, intrapersonal, mathematical, linguistic, existential, and naturalist knowing, so that they might be seen and understood for the deep and authentic intelligences they are.

When I was in school, subjects such as visual and performing arts were known as electives or "soft subjects," meaning you didn't HAVE to take them; they were not "hard" like the sciences and mathematics. As time has passed, many of these performing and visual arts have been removed from the K-12 curriculum in favor of more academic subjects. Locally, there are schools that have to resort to bake sales to pay the salary of the art teacher. This is an embarrassingly sad development in light of what we've learned about the breadth and depth of true intelligence.

If we cannot change this systemically, we can at least bring a taste of it into our own classrooms. Music can make a lesson come alive. Art can provide a welcome venue for expression of an aspiring painter. Assignments can include an intrapersonal aspect. Students can choose just once in a while how they will show what they know. Write your ideas below for going beyond reading and writing. Every once in a while, let them express their natural intelligence.

....

....

....

....

....

....

....

....

You cannot step in the same river twice.

Heraclitus, a pre-Socratic philosopher, is famous for his insistence on ever-present change in the universe, as stated in the famous saying, "No man ever steps in the same river twice."

And here we are. Same classroom, same textbook, same room arrangement, same calendar on the wall, same faces you saw yesterday—it might lead you to think it's all pretty much the same. But the truth is, as teacher, YOU are the distinguisher; you are the one who sees and discerns how today is different than yesterday. Sometimes it's a new topic, sometimes it's a change in the weather or a surprising room arrangement, and sometimes it is a barely perceptible change.

It is our challenge in this service of teaching and learning to alert and awaken ourselves to what could, should, might be, or just is unique about this day, this lesson, this dialogue. Maybe you want to draw out a student who has been super shy. Maybe you want to tweak the lesson to contain a poem. Perhaps you will sit in a circle on the floor. Or view together a TED talk that you watched recently. Find ways to mix it up and keep the class from being lulled into the seeming sameness. How might you make today its own?

Do they know what you believe, what you fear?

As mentioned before, teaching can be an isolating profession, and it can be very tempting to join in that isolation, keeping your teaching life very private. So the doubts you have about your own teaching don't get mentioned, just harbored in your heart and soul. The joys you have about teaching may also go unexpressed, as there may be little space and opportunity for sharing these. It is not within the typical venue of schools to offer space and place to come together around our teaching experiences, and we lose a great deal because of this. The truth is we may actually be losing our own stories.

Both the vulnerabilities and the spectacular moments of inspiration that teachers experience, are meant to live together. When we keep ourselves from the community we could be a part of, we lose a precious commodity. What do you believe right now about yourself as teacher? As Parker Palmer so importantly asked, "Who is the *Self* who teaches" in your classroom? What is your next longing on your teaching path? With whom can you share this? Open the door. Find them. Let them know.

Consider below what you are willing to share with another teacher and how you might begin.

....

....

....

....

....

....

....

....

....

....

....

....

....

....

....

The question that didn't want to be answered.

How many times have you heard a teacher ask, "Any questions?" And how many times have you heard stone-cold silence in response? Too often, we just move on because no one has had "any questions." So, how 'bout we get rid of *that* question?

Let's find a hundred different ways to ask, so that children will engage with the question, will think in response, will touch their own curiosity, and will come alive instead of tuning out.

Give it a try.

- We just talked about the _____.
- What do you think is fascinating about it?
- Where do you believe the _____ originated?
- If you were to identify the most important fact that holds this altogether, what would it be?

- Why on earth would we need to study _____?
- What will it help us do, know, or solve?
- How is what we just studied like what we studied last week?

Use the space below to begin your list of 100 questions to engage students. Any questions? ☺

....

....

....

....

....

....

....

....

....

....

What part of yourself?

Rachel Naomi Remen (1999) spoke at the "Spirituality in Education Conference" I attended in Boulder, Colorado. At the beginning of her presentation, she told about seminars she facilitated for doctors and how she was concerned about the human element being left out of medical training, methodology and practice. She would begin the first session of these seminars with:

What part of yourself do you feel you are or might be losing as you work in this profession?

She found that the doctors were able to quickly identify and share with her and one another an aspect or quality of themselves they were afraid they might lose while serving in the medical profession. Answers included a loss of sense of humor, joy, and balance in their lives. Wow! What a wake-up call it was. This question has lived in me since and become a touchstone, a guiding presence by which to check myself.

To consider where I was fully alive in my teaching and where I was hiding seemed an important exploration. It was so tempting to become the "role" of teacher, and yet I also wanted to be "real." Every once in a while, I found myself asking, "Where is Patty?" And sometimes, to my dismay, I was not always sure.

For me, the loss was coming in the area of humor. I was taking my job so seriously I ignored the absurdity of some of it and missed the pure joy of learning with my students. I found myself laughing less and worrying more. This was an imbalance I did not want to sustain. So I would reorient, read a book by Maya Angelou, take a long walk with Alee along the Big Thompson River, or journal to find myself again.

And how about you, dear teacher? What comes to mind as you consider:

"What part of yourself do you feel you are or might be losing as you work in this profession called TEACHER?"

Write your first response below. Read the question and the answer aloud. Touch the words that you've written.

Hold that part of you as sacred. Promise to do what you can to protect, preserve, and promote that unique essence of yourself. The world needs you healthy, whole, and integrated. The kids are counting on you.

....
....
....
....
....
....
....
....
....
....
....

Take good care,
Patty Lee

References

Angelou, M. (1978) *And Still I Rise*. Random House.

Baldwin, C. (1998) *Calling the Circle*. Bantam Books.

Covey, S. (1989) *The Seven Habits of Highly Effective People*. Simon & Schuster.

Elmore, R. (2011) *I Used to Think...and Now I Think*. Harvard Education Press.

Gardner, H. (1983) *Frames of Mind*. Basic Books.

Graves, D. (2001) *The Energy to Teach*. Heinemann.

Markova, D. (2000) *I Will not Die an Unlived Life*. Conair Press.

Moorman, C. (2001) *Spirit Whisperers*. Personal Power Press.

Palmer, P. (1998) *The Courage to Teach*. Jossey-Bass.

Schön, D. (1983) *The Reflective Practitioner: How Professionals Think in Action*. Basic Books.

www.ingramcontent.com/pod-product-compliance
Lightning Source LLC
LaVergne TN
LVHW011243080426
835509LV00005B/615